SRA

LANGUAGE for LEARNING

Behavioral Objectives Booklet

Siegfried Engelmann   Jean Osborn

Reviewer

Dr. Betsy Loveday

Educational Consultant

Knoxville, TN

SRAonline.com

Send all inquiries to this address:
SRA/McGraw-Hill
4400 Easton Commons
Columbus, OH 43219

SBN: 978-0-07-609431-8
MHID: 0-07-609431-6

8 9 10   QVS   16 15 14

The McGraw-Hill Companies

LANGUAGE for LEARNING
Behavioral Objectives

INTRODUCTION

A major premise of the *Language for Learning* program is that children must understand the language of instruction. The children's social language may be fully adequate for their lives outside the classroom, but if they do not understand the meaning of the language of the teacher and classroom and the language encountered in the textbook, they are likely to fail in school.

Language for Learning is designed to teach the language of instruction. The program is based upon analysis of skills and concepts the child must understand to follow the variety of basic instructions presented both in workbooks and by the teacher. It consists of carefully programmed sequences of exercises grouped into daily lessons, including teacher-directed activities and independent seatwork. These lessons provide for continual review of all the concepts and skills that are taught, as well as their application in problem-solving situations.

HOW TO USE THIS BOOKLET

This booklet is intended to give a comprehensive picture of *Language for Learning* by focusing on general curriculum goals of the program and specific behavioral objectives to be achieved by the individual child.

Scope and Sequence Chart

The Scope and Sequence Chart for *Language for Learning* (pages 14–15) provides a quick overview of the program. The chart lists the various tracks (skills) that are taught and the range of lessons for each track.

Objectives

This booklet is organized into major skill areas, or tracks. Tracks are grouped into six categories as shown on the Scope and Sequence Chart.

For each track or subtrack, the following information is provided:

- The "purpose of the track" is the general curriculum objective. For example, the purpose of the track for Concept Applications is to teach the child to apply previously learned skills to solve problems in a new context.

- The "behavioral objective" is the kind of performance that can be expected from the child who has mastered the skill. For example, the behavioral objective for Concept Applications is as follows: When presented a problem using two or more concepts that have been taught, the child is able to solve the problem by answering questions about a picture.

- The activities are specific kinds of exercises the child performs in order to master the skill. For example, in Concept Applications the concepts are listed along with the number of the lesson where each activity first appears. In this way, the teacher can see the progression of skill development.

I. Actions

A. Beginning Actions

Range of lessons 1–22

Purpose of the track
To teach the child to identify and perform simple actions

Behavioral Objectives
When directed to perform a simple action, the child is able to perform the action, label the action, and make a complete statement describing the action.

The child is asked to

First appears in

- perform an action and describe it in a phrase. — Lesson 1
- perform an action and describe it both in a phrase and in a complete statement, following the teacher's lead. — Lesson 7
- perform an action and describe it in a phrase and in a statement. — Lesson 10

B. Parts of the Body

Range of lessons 4–41

Purpose of the track
To teach the child to identify parts of the body and perform simple actions involving the parts of the body

Behavioral Objectives
When directed to perform an action involving a part of the body, the child is able to perform the action, describe it in a phrase, and make a complete statement using the name of the body part.

The child is asked to

First appears in

- touch a part of the body. — Lesson 4
  > *For example—Teacher: I can touch my head. Watch.*
  > *(Touch your head.)*
  > *Everybody, touch your head.*
- describe the action in a phrase. — Lesson 4
  > *For example—Teacher: Touch your head.*
  > *What are you doing?*
  > *Child: Touching my head.*
- describe the action in a complete statement. — Lesson 7
  > *For example—Teacher: Say the whole thing.*
  > *Child: I am touching my head.*

C. Pictures

Range of lessons 17–42

Purpose of the track
To teach the child to describe pictured actions

Behavioral Objectives
When shown pictures, the child is able to describe the illustrated actions in complete affirmative and negative statements.

The child is asked to

First appears in

- describe illustrated actions with affirmative statements. — Lesson 17
  > *For example—This dog is sitting.*

- describe illustrated actions with affirmative and negative statements.   Lesson 24

  For example—This girl is eating.

  This girl is not eating.

D. Pronouns

Range of lessons 23–52

Purpose of the track
To teach the child to use pronouns

Behavioral Objectives
When one or more persons perform an action, the child is able to describe the action in a statement using the appropriate pronoun or pronouns.

The child is asked to use the following pronoun or pronouns:

	First appears in		*First appears in*
I-you	Lesson 23	she-her	Lesson 37
you-your	Lesson 24	he-his	Lesson 38
I-my	Lesson 26	they	Lesson 45
we	Lesson 28	our	Lesson 51

E. Tense

Range of lessons 55–150

Purpose of the track
To teach the child the concepts of past, present, and future tenses, as well as the words denoting the different tenses

Behavioral Objectives—Past and Present Tense
1. **When an action has been performed with an object, the child is able to make statements about the object using the past and present tenses.**

The child is asked to

	First appears in

- describe an object in statements using the past and present tenses.   Lesson 55

  For example—This glass was full.

  This glass is not full.

- state where an object was before it was moved.   Lesson 55

  For example—The glass was on the floor.

- state where an object is and where it was before the teacher moved it.   Lesson 56

  For example—Teacher: Where is the book?

  Child: On the paper.

  Teacher: (Hold the book over the paper.)

  *Where **was** the book?*

  Child: On the paper.

2. **When an action is being done or was done, the child is able to describe it in a phrase.**

The child is asked to   *First appears in*

- describe in a phrase an action that is being done or was done.   Lesson 120

  For example—Teacher: What is he doing?

  Child: Standing up.

  Teacher: What was he doing before he stood up?

  Child: Sitting down.

Behavioral Objectives—Future Tense
When directed to perform an action, the child is able to perform and describe the action in a statement using future tense.

The child is asked to

- describe in a complete statement an action that will take place in the future.

    For example—Teacher: What will she do?
        Child: She will stand up.

First appears in
Lesson 121

F. Tense—Pictures

Range of lessons
59–98

Purpose of the track
To teach the child to describe pictured actions using different tenses

Behavioral Objectives
When shown pictures of events in a time sequence, the child is able to make statements in the appropriate tense about the actions in each picture.

The child is asked to

- describe pictures in statements using the past and present tenses.

    For example—(Picture 1) The cat is on the floor.
        (Picture 2) The cat is on the couch.
            The cat was on the floor.

First appears in
Lesson 59

G. Actions—Review

Range of lessons
51–150

Purpose of the track
To provide a continual review of the concepts and statement patterns taught in the program
To provide the child with opportunities to incorporate into action exercises the concepts learned in other tracks

Behavioral Objectives
1. **When asked to perform an action applying concepts taught in the program, the child is able to follow directions and perform the action correctly.**
2. **When asked to describe actions, performed or pictured, the child is able to make complete statements using the appropriate tense.**

II. Descriptions of Objects
A. Object Identification

Range of lessons
1–8

Purpose of the track
To teach the child to label common objects

Behavioral Objectives
When shown pictures of common objects, the child is able to identify each object with a noun and the article *a*.

The child is asked to

- identify common objects with a noun and the article *a*.

    For example—A tree.

First appears in
Lesson 1

B. Identity Statements

Range of lessons
3–38

Purpose of the track
To teach the child to make complete statements about common objects

Behavioral Objectives Booklet **5**

Behavioral Objectives

1. **When shown pictures of common objects, the child is able to identify each object using the article *a* or *an* correctly and make a complete statement about the object.**

The child is asked to

- label an object using the article *a* and the noun and make a complete identification statement.

    For example—This is a dog.

- label an object using the article *an* and the noun and make a complete identification statement.

    For example—This is an eraser.

2. **When asked questions about pictures of common objects, the child is able to respond correctly with *yes* or *no* and with complete affirmative or negative statements.**

The child is asked to

- respond with *yes* or *no* to a question beginning with *is*.
- respond with an affirmative statement to a question about an object.
- respond with a negative statement to a question about an object.

    For example—Teacher: What is this?

    Child: A horse.

    Teacher: Say the whole thing.

    Child: This is a horse.

    Teacher: Is this a dog?

    Child: No.

    Teacher: Say the whole thing.

    Child: This is not a dog.

	First appears in
label an object using the article *a*...	Lesson 3
label an object using the article *an*...	Lesson 21
respond with *yes* or *no*...	Lesson 15
respond with an affirmative statement...	Lesson 15
respond with a negative statement...	Lesson 20

C. Common Objects
Range of lessons 7–33

Purpose of the track
To teach the child the names of common classroom objects and to make statements about these objects

Behavioral Objectives
When the teacher touches different objects in the classroom, the child is able to identify the objects and make a complete statement about each one.

The child is asked to
- label a classroom object and make a complete statement about each one.

    For example—Teacher: (Touch a chalkboard.) What is this?

    Child: A chalkboard.

    Teacher: Say the whole thing.

    Child: This is a chalkboard.

First appears in Lesson 7

D. Missing Objects
Range of lessons 23–34

Purpose of the track
To teach the child to identify a missing object when one is removed from a group

Behavioral Objectives

When the teacher removes an object from a group, the child is able to identify which object is missing.

The child is asked to
- identify in a phrase which object is missing.

First appears in
Lesson 23

E. Plurals _____

Range of lessons 51–79

Purpose of the track
To teach the child the difference between singular and plural forms of nouns and verbs

Behavioral Objectives—Actions
1. **When given a direction containing either a singular or a plural noun, the child is able to recognize whether the word refers to one or more than one.**

The child is asked to
- discriminate between singular and plural words used by the teacher.
- perform an action involving one or more than one part of the body.
  > For example—Hold up your hands.
  >   Hold up your hand.

First appears in
Lesson 51
Lesson 52

2. **When directed to point to one or more than one object, the child is able to describe the action in a statement using the correct singular or plural noun form.**

The child is asked to
- point to one or more than one part of the body and describe the action in a statement.

First appears in
Lesson 60

Behavioral Objectives—Pictures
1. **When shown a picture, the child is able to describe the picture using the correct singular and plural forms of the noun.**

The child is asked to
- use a singular or plural noun to describe a picture.

First appears in
Lesson 54

2. **When shown a picture, the child is able to make a statement containing singular or plural nouns to describe the picture.**

The child is asked to
- make a statement using a singular or plural noun to describe one or more than one object in a picture.

First appears in
Lesson 62

F. Opposites _____

Range of lessons 24–150

Purpose of the track
To teach the child pairs of words that are opposites, demonstrate the meanings of these words, and teach the comparative forms

Behavioral Objectives
1. **When asked a question about one word of an opposite pair, the child is able to recognize the meaning of the word and answer the question correctly.**

The child is asked to

- answer a yes-or-no question containing one word of an opposite pair.

First appears in
Lesson 24

> *For example—Teacher: Is this glass full?*
> *Child: Yes.*

2. **When shown a picture, the child is able to describe the picture with a statement containing one word of an opposite pair or one word of an opposite pair with "not."**

> *For example—This glass is full.*
> *This glass is not full.*

The child is asked to answer questions containing one word of an opposite pair:

	First appears in		*First appears in*
full/not full	Lesson 24	long/not long	Lesson 50
wet/not wet	Lesson 30	old/not old	Lesson 58
big/not big	Lesson 37		

Behavioral Objectives—Opposites

When shown a picture, the child is able to describe the picture with a statement containing one word of an opposite pair.

The child is asked to use the following opposites:

	First appears in		*First appears in*
full/empty	Lesson 41	awake/asleep	Lesson 130
big/small	Lesson 43	late/early	Lesson 132
wet/dry	Lesson 45	fast/slow	Lesson 134
long/short	Lesson 53	sick/well	Lesson 136
old/young	Lesson 60	hard/soft	Lesson 141
tall/short	Lesson 91	daytime/nighttime	Lesson 143
hot/cold	Lesson 123	clean/dirty	Lesson 145
sad/happy	Lesson 125	lose/win	Lesson 147
open/close	Lesson 128	noisy/quiet	Lesson 149

G. Comparatives

Range of lessons 131–146

Purpose of the track
To teach the child the comparative forms of opposite words learned

Behavioral Objectives

1. **When directed to compare pictured objects, the child is able to answer a question about the comparative relationship between the objects.**

The child is asked to

- answer question about the comparative relationship between objects.

First appears in
Lesson 131

> *For example—Teacher: Which is bigger, the ball or the cup?*
> *Child: The ball.*

2. **When asked to compare pictured objects, the child is able to make a complete statement using the comparative form to show the relationship.**

The child is asked to

- describe pictured objects in complete statements using the comparative form to show the relationship.

First appears in
Lesson 131

III. Information and Background Knowledge

A. Names

Range of lessons 1–23

Purpose of the track

To teach the child the difference between first name and whole name and teach the names of the children in the group

Behavioral Objectives

When working in a group, the child is able to say his or her own name and identify by name every child in the group.

The child is asked to	*First appears in*
• say his or her first name and the first name of every child in the group.	Lesson 1
• say his or her own whole name and the whole name of every child in the group.	Lesson 15

B. Basic Information

Range of lessons 1–34

Purpose of the track

To teach the child the name of the teacher, school, city or town, and state in which the child lives

Behavioral Objectives

When directed, the child is able to respond with the teacher's name, the name of the school, and the name of the city or town in which he or she lives.

The child is asked to	*First appears in*
• say the name of his or her teacher and school.	Lesson 1
• say the name of the city or town in which he or she lives.	Lesson 27

C. Days of the Week

Range of lesson 35–74

Purpose of the track

To teach the child to name the seven days of the week in order

Behavioral Objectives

When directed, the child is able to name the seven days of the week in order.

The child is asked to	*First appears in*
• state that there are seven days in a week.	Lesson 35
• name the days of the week in order.	Lesson 41

D. Months of the Year

Range of lessons 92–115

Purpose of the track

To teach the child the names of the months of the year in order

Behavioral Objectives

When directed, the child is able to name the months of the year in order and distinguish the difference in naming the days of the week and the months of the year.

The child is asked to

- state that there are twelve months in a year.   Lesson 92
- name the months of the year in order.   Lesson 104
- name the months of the year and the days of the week in order.   Lesson 104

E. Seasons _____ Range of lessons 128–138

Purpose of the track

To teach the child the names of the four seasons and to describe the characteristics of each season

Behavioral Objectives

When shown pictures illustrating the seasons, the child is able to name the seasons and describe the characteristics of each season.

The child is asked to   *First appears in*

- recognize and name *winter* and describe its characteristics.   Lesson 132
- recognize and name *spring* and describe its characteristics.   Lesson 133
- recognize and name *fall* and describe its characteristics.   Lesson 134
- recognize and name *summer* and describe its characteristics.   Lesson 135

F. Part/Whole Relationships _____ Range of lessons 28–125

Purpose of the track

To teach the names of common objects, the names of the parts and their relation to the whole, and the function of the object

Behavioral Objectives

When shown a real or pictured object, the child is able to identify the object, name its parts, and state how the object is used.

The child is asked to identify the following common objects:

	First appears in		*First appears in*
head	Lesson 28	body	Lesson 86
table	Lesson 30	house	Lesson 91
pencil	Lesson 32	shoe	Lesson 96
toothbrush	Lesson 35	nail	Lesson 101
elephant	Lesson 41	pin	Lesson 102
wagon	Lesson 44	chair	Lesson 106
tree	Lesson 48	cabinet	Lesson 111
umbrella	Lesson 59	hammer	Lesson 111
car	Lesson 65	saw	Lesson 112
flower	Lesson 68	broom	Lesson 117
coat	Lesson 79	belt	Lesson 117

G. Materials _____ Range of lessons 62–148

Purpose of the track

To teach the child to identify the materials of which common objects are or can be made

Behavioral Objectives

1. **When presented with an object, the child is able to discriminate between the name of the part and the material of which the part is made.**

The child is asked to
- identify the part and the material of which the part is made.

For example—A shirt.

Teacher: (Touch a button.) What is the name of this part?
Child: A button.
Teacher: What's it made of?
Child: Plastic.

First appears in
Lesson 62

2. **When shown a picture of different objects made of a given material, the child is able to name each object and recall the names of the objects when the picture is removed.**

The child is asked to
- name pictured objects made of a given material.

First appears in
Lesson 70

3. **When presented with the name of a material, the child is able to name objects that can be made of this material.**

The child is asked to
- name objects made of a specified material.

First appears in
Lesson 75

For example—Teacher: Let's see who can name at least three things made of wood.

4. **When asked what materials could be used to make a given object, the child is able to name several possibilities.**

The child is asked to
- name materials of which a given object could be made.

First appears in
Lesson 76

The child is asked to identify the following materials:

	First appears in		*First appears in*
cloth	Lesson 62	glass	Lesson 72
paper (piece of)	Lesson 62	metal	Lesson 83
plastic	Lesson 62	concrete	Lesson 89
graphite	Lesson 64	rubber	Lesson 106
wood	Lesson 64	paper	Lesson 121
rubber (eraser)	Lesson 64	brick	Lesson 126
leather	Lesson 66		

H. Common Information

Range of lessons 71–150

Purpose of the track
To teach the child vocabulary for occupations, places, and natural phenomena

Behavioral Objectives—Occupations
When the teacher shows a picture of or names a person in a certain occupation (such as a dentist or firefighter), the child is able to state what the person is called and give a simple description of the person's occupation.

The child is asked to recognize the following occupations:

	First appears in		First appears in
dentist	Lesson 71	passenger	Lesson 118
firefighter	Lesson 79	painter	Lesson 125
teacher	Lesson 80	pilot	Lesson 132
carpenter	Lesson 95	lumberjack	Lesson 134
doctor	Lesson 107	librarian	Lesson 137
nurse	Lesson 108	customer	Lesson 140
patient	Lesson 109	waiter	Lesson 141
police officer	Lesson 113	mechanic	Lesson 146
driver	Lesson 117		

Behavioral Objectives—Places

When the teacher shows a picture of or names a place (such as city or jungle), the child is able to name and give a simple description of the place.

The child is asked to recognize the following places:

	First appears in		First appears in
city	Lesson 71	ship	Lesson 121
farm	Lesson 73	grocery store	Lesson 122
store	Lesson 74	airport	Lesson 131
forest	Lesson 85	fire station	Lesson 133
orchard	Lesson 94	library	Lesson 136
jungle	Lesson 116	restaurant	Lesson 138
beach	Lesson 120	garage	Lesson 147

Behavioral Objectives—Natural Phenomena

When the teacher shows a picture of or names a natural phenomenon (such as sky or sun), the child is able to name and give a simple description of the phenomenon.

The child is asked to recognize the following natural phenomena:

	First appears in		First appears in
land	Lesson 75	clouds	Lesson 75
sky	Lesson 75	Earth	Lesson 83
sun	Lesson 75	ocean	Lesson 87

I. Locations

Range of lessons 127–150

Purpose of the track

To teach locations and the people associated with these locations

Behavioral Objectives

When shown a picture of a location (previously taught in the common information track), the child is able to name the location, identify the people and objects found in the location, and identify the functions of the people and objects.

The child is asked to recognize the following locations:

	First appears in		First appears in
farm	Lesson 127	jungle	Lesson 141
grocery store	Lesson 129	airport	Lesson 143
dentist's office	Lesson 132	fire station	Lesson 145
doctor's office	Lesson 133	library	Lesson 147
city	Lesson 136	garage	Lesson 147
ocean	Lesson 138	restaurant	Lesson 149
forest	Lesson 138		

IV. Instructional Words and Problem-Solving Concepts

A. Spatial and Temporal Relations

Range of lessons 17–48

Purpose of the track
To teach the child the vocabulary needed for temporal sequencing skills

Behavioral Objectives—First, Next
When presented a two-action sequence using the words first and next, the child is able to identify and perform the actions in the correct order.

The child is asked to   **First appears in**

- identify *first* and *next* actions.   Lesson 17

    For example—Teacher: My turn. Here I go. (Clap. Pause. Smile.)
                        What did I do first?
                Child: Clapped.
                Teacher: What did I do next?
                Child: Smiled.

- perform actions in *first* and *next* sequence.   Lesson 17

    For example—Teacher: Your turn. First you'll touch your ear. Next you'll
                        smile. Get ready. (Signal. The children respond.)

Scope and Sequence Charts
The Scope and Sequence Charts display the content of *Language for Learning* and the sequence of instruction. Each track is represented by a line; the starting and ending lessons of each track can be determined by referring to the lesson numbers at the top of the page. It is important to understand, however, that a track line indicates that the track's exercises appear frequently during the range of lessons indicated but not necessarily in every single lesson.

In addition, the Scope and Sequence Charts do not illustrate one of the strong features of *Language for Learning*: after concepts are presented in their own tracks, the children apply them in other, more advanced tracks.

Language for Learning Scope and Sequence

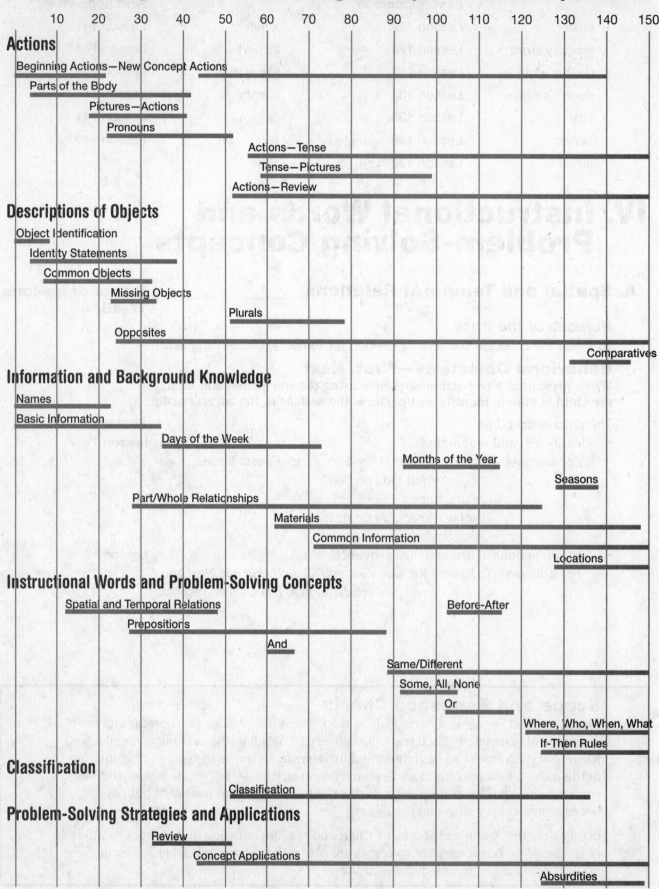

10 20 30 40 50 60 70 80 90 100 110 120 130 140 150

Actions

Beginning Actions—New Concept Actions

Parts of the Body

Pictures—Actions

Pronouns

Actions—Tense

Tense—Pictures

Actions—Review

Descriptions of Objects

Object Identification

Identity Statements

Common Objects

Missing Objects

Plurals

Opposites

Comparatives

Information and Background Knowledge

Names

Basic Information

Days of the Week

Months of the Year

Seasons

Part/Whole Relationships

Materials

Common Information

Locations

Instructional Words and Problem-Solving Concepts

Spatial and Temporal Relations

Prepositions

And

Before-After

Same/Different

Some, All, None

Or

Where, Who, When, What

If-Then Rules

Classification

Classification

Problem-Solving Strategies and Applications

Review

Concept Applications

Absurdities

Workbook Scope and Sequence

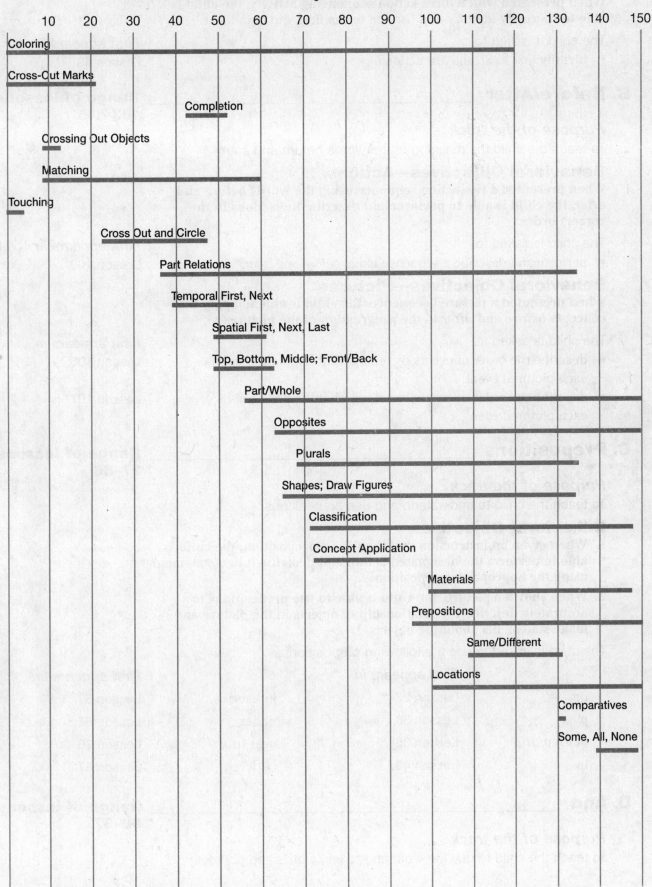

Behavioral Objectives—First, Next, Last

When presented with a three-action sequencing activity, the child is able to correctly identify and use the terms first, next, and last.

The child is asked to
*   identify *first, next,* and *last* actions.

First appears in
Lesson 39

B. Before/After

Range of lessons 103–115

Purpose of the track
To teach the child the meaning of the words *before* and *after*

Behavioral Objectives—Actions
When presented a two-action sequence using the words *before* and *after,* the child is able to perform and describe the actions in the correct order.

The child is asked to
*   perform and describe a sequence using *before* and *after.*

First appears in
Lesson 103

Behavioral Objectives—Pictures
When presented a pictured sequence, the child is able to apply the concepts *before* and *after* to the progression of the pictures.

The child is asked to
*   describe the order of events by telling what happens *after* each pictured event.
*   describe the order of events by telling what happens *before* each pictured event.

First appears in
Lesson 106

Lesson 107

C. Prepositions

Range of lessons 27–88

Purpose of the track
To teach the child to understand and use prepositions

Behavioral Objectives
1. When given an instruction that involves a preposition, the child is able to perform the designated action and describe it in a statement using the appropriate preposition.
2. When shown a picture, the child is able to use prepositions to accurately describe the relationship of objects in the picture and make statements about the objects.

The child is asked to use the following prepositions:

	First appears in		*First appears in*
on	Lesson 27	in back of	Lesson 57
over	Lesson 30	under	Lesson 67
in front of	Lesson 35	next to	Lesson 76
in	Lesson 46	between	Lesson 87

D. And

Range of lessons 60–67

Purpose of the track
To teach the child to use the word *and* to join words and phrases

Behavioral Objectives

When asked to perform two actions, the child is able to perform them and describe the actions in a statement using *and*.

The child is asked to
- make a statement using *and* to join phrases describing two actions that have been performed.

First appears in
Lesson 60

E. Same/different

Range of lessons 89–150

Purpose of the track

To teach the child to use the concepts *same* and *different* when describing characteristics of objects or actions of people and animals

Behavioral Objectives

1. When the teacher performs a specified action, the child is able to perform the same action.

The child is asked to
- perform the same action the teacher performs.

First appears in
Lesson 89

2. When the child performs a specified action, the child is able to recognize whether the teacher performs the same action or a different action.

The child is asked to
- perform an action, watch the teacher's action, and then state whether the teacher's action is the same or different.
- perform an action and direct the teacher to perform the same action.

First appears in
Lesson 113

Lesson 113

Behavioral Objectives—Pictures

1. When shown pictures of objects, the child is able to recognize that objects that are not identical but have the same name can be described as the same.

The child is asked to
- recognize that things are the same because they have the same name.

First appears in
Lesson 92

2. When shown pictures of objects, the child is able to recognize that objects may be the same in more than one way.

The child is asked to
- identify objects as the same because they have the same name or because they are doing or wearing the same thing.

First appears in
Lesson 96

Behavioral Objectives—Class

When the teacher names objects in the same class, the child is able to identify the class in which the objects belong.

The child is asked to
- identify common classifications.

First appears in
Lesson 99

Behavioral Objectives—Same

When the teacher names objects, the child is able to describe them as the same because they have the same function, are found in the same place, or have the same parts.

The child is asked to
- state in a phrase what two objects do that is the same.

    For example—Teacher: A boat and a fish. What do they do that's the same?

    Child: Go in the water.

First appears in
Lesson 102

- name the same place in which two objects are found.   Lesson 105

  > *For example—Teacher: An airplane and a bird. You see them both in*
  > *the same place. Everybody, what place is that?*
  > *Child: The sky.*

- name the same parts in two objects.   Lesson 148

Behavioral Objectives—Different
When the teacher names two objects, the child is able to compare the objects and describe how they are the same and how they are different.

The child is asked to   *First appears in*

- describe in a statement how two objects are different.   Lesson 118
- describe in a statement how two objects are the same and how they are different.   Lesson 119

F. Some, All, None _____   **Range of lessons 92–105**

Purpose of the track
To teach the meaning of the words *some, all,* and *none*

Behavioral Objectives—Actions
1. **When the teacher holds up zero to ten fingers, the child is able to recognize when *some, all,* or *none* of the fingers are up.**

The child is asked to   *First appears in*

- respond *yes* or *no* when the teacher holds up various numbers of fingers and asks, "Am I holding up all of my fingers?"   Lesson 92
- respond correctly when the teacher holds up various numbers of fingers and asks, "Is this *all* of my fingers or *some* of my fingers?"   Lesson 93
- respond correctly when the teacher holds up various numbers of fingers and asks, "Is this *all* of my fingers or *some* of my fingers or *none* of my fingers?"   Lesson 99
2. **When given a direction, the child is able to respond correctly by holding up all, some, or none of his or her fingers and describe the action.**

The child is asked to   *First appears in*

- hold up *all* of his or her fingers and describe the action.   Lesson 92
- hold up *all* or *some* of his or her fingers and describe the action.   Lesson 93
- hold up *all, some,* or *none* of his or her fingers and describe the action.   Lesson 99

Behavioral Objectives—Pictures
When the teacher presents pictures, the child is able to use the words *some, all,* and *none* to answer questions.

The child is asked to   *First appears in*

- state whether the teacher is covering *some, all,* or *none* of the objects in the picture.   Lesson 96

G. Or _____   **Range of lessons 102–118**

Purpose of the track
To teach the child to use the word *or* in a statement of alternative possibilities

Behavioral Objectives—Or
When the teacher says he or she is going to do one of several actions, the child is able to understand that these are alternative possibilities and describe them in a phrase using *or*.

The child is asked to
- describe several possibilities in a phrase containing *or*.

> *For example—Teacher: I'm going to frown or smile.*
> *What am I going to do?*
> *Child: Frown or smile.*

First appears in
Lesson 102

Behavioral Objectives—Maybe

When the teacher gives alternative possibilities that he or she will perform, the child is able to discriminate between the possible action and all other actions.

The child is asked to

First appears in

- respond *maybe* when the teacher asks whether he or she will do one of the possible actions.

Lesson 102

- respond *no* when the teacher asks whether he or she will do any other action.

Lesson 102

> *For example—*
>
> Teacher: I'm going to frown or smile.   Teacher: Am I going to read
>   What am I going to do?   a book?
> Child: Frown or smile.   Child: No.
> Teacher: Am I going to frown?   Teacher: Am I going to smile?
> Child: Maybe.   Child: Maybe.

H. Where, Who, When, What

Range of lessons 121–150

Purpose of the track

To teach the child to discriminate between and answer *where, who, when,* and *what* questions

Behavioral Objectives

When shown a picture, the child is able to answer *where, who, when,* and *what* questions about the picture.

The child is asked to

First appears in

- respond to *when* questions.

Lesson 121

- respond to *where* questions (previously introduced in prepositions track). Lesson 121
- respond to *what* and *who* questions (previously introduced in actions track).

Lesson 121

I. If-Then Rules

Range of lessons 125–150

Purpose of the track

To teach the child the meaning of if-then statements and introduce the child to deductive reasoning

Behavioral Objectives

1. **When presented with a command, the child is able to respond only if a specified condition is fulfilled.**

The child is asked to

First appears in

- respond to a command only if a specified condition is fulfilled.

Lesson 125

> *For example—Teacher: If the teacher says "go," touch your head.*

Behavioral Objectives Booklet **19**

2. **When shown a group of pictures, the child is able to apply an if-then rule to pick the picture or pictures that fulfill the condition.**

The child is asked to
* select the picture or pictures that fulfill the *if* part of the if-then rule.

First appears in
Lesson 126

3. **When presented with a series of pictures, the child is able to construct an if-then rule based upon the details of the pictures.**

The child is asked to
* make an if-then rule by observing features of a picture.

First appears in
Lesson 137

V. Classification

Classification _____

Range of lessons
51–136

Purpose of the track

To teach the child common classification terms and the names of objects found in each class and teach the child to group objects that share common features

Behavioral Objectives—Pictures

When shown a picture and given the word for a common classification, the child is able to recognize and tell in complete statements whether or not objects belong in the classification.

The child is asked to
* recognize and tell in complete statements whether or not objects belong in the classification.
    For example—This is a vehicle.
    This is not a vehicle.

First appears in
Lesson 51

The child is asked to recognize the following classifications:

	First appears in		*First appears in*
vehicles	Lesson 51	buildings	Lesson 101
food	Lesson 61	plants	Lesson 111
containers	Lesson 71	tools	Lesson 122
clothing	Lesson 74	furniture	Lesson 133
animals	Lesson 83		

Behavioral Objectives—Names of Objects within a Classification

When a common classification word is given, the child is able to identify and make statements about the objects that belong in the classification.

The child is asked to
* recognize and tell in complete statements objects that belong in a given classification.
    For example—This furniture is a bookcase.
    This tree is not a vehicle.

First appears in
Lesson 51

Behavioral Objectives—Classification Rules

1. **When a classification rule is presented, the child is able to use the rule to determine whether or not an object belongs in the specified classification.**

The child is asked to
- use a classification rule to determine whether or not an object belongs in the specified classification.

First appears in
Lesson 76

    *For example—**Rule:** If it is made to take you places, it's a vehicle.*
    Teacher: Can an apple take you places?
    Child: No.
    Teacher: So is an apple a vehicle?
    Child: No.

2. **When the teacher specifies a classification and then names objects, the child is able to state whether or not an object belongs in this classification.**

The child is asked to
- identify objects that belong in classifications previously learned in picture exercises.

First appears in
Lesson 70

VI. Problem-Solving Strategies and Applications

A. Review

Range of lessons 33–52

Purpose of the track
To provide new contexts, new uses, and new statements for the concepts taught in the various tracks of the program

Behavioral Objectives
When shown a picture, the child is able to answer questions and describe objects and actions in the picture.

The child is asked to
- answer questions and describe objects and actions in a picture.

First appears in
Lesson 33

    For example—Teacher: Look at the picture. Who is wearing a hat?
    Child: The dog.
    Teacher: Yes, the dog.
       Look at the car. What is sitting in the car?
    Child: The dog.
    Teacher: Yes, the dog is sitting in the car.
       Look at the tree. Who is chopping down the tree?
    Child: The man.
    Teacher: Yes, the man is chopping down the tree.
       Look at the dog again. What is the dog doing?
    Child: Sitting in the car.
    Teacher: Say the whole thing about what the dog is doing.
    Child: The dog is sitting in the car.
    Teacher: Look at the man again. What is the man doing?
    Child: Chopping down the tree.
    Teacher: Say the whole thing about what the man is doing.
    Child: The man is chopping down the tree.

B. Concept Applications

**Range of lessons
43–150**

Purpose of the track
To teach the child to apply previously learned skills to solve problems in a new context

Behavioral Objectives
When presented a problem using two or more concepts that have been taught, the child is able to solve the problem by answering questions about the picture.

The child is asked to apply the following concepts in problem solving:

	First appears in
color and actions	Lesson 43
opposites and actions	Lesson 49
opposites, actions, and parts	Lesson 64
descriptive terms, future tense, and actions	Lesson 66
classification, parts, future tense, and plurals	Lesson 68
future tense, actions, multiple descriptive terms, opposites, and parts	Lesson 84
same, only, future tense, and descriptive terms	Lesson 100
every, actions, and descriptive terms	Lesson 105
or, classification, future tense, and actions	Lesson 111
future tense, actions, prepositions, and *or*	Lesson 112
all, part/whole, and prepositions	Lesson 125
prepositions, classification, and comparatives	Lesson 136
all, some, none, tense, and plurals	Lesson 146

C. Absurdities

**Range of lessons
125–149**

Purpose of the track
To teach the child to recognize an absurd situation by applying logical analysis

Behavioral Objectives—Function
When asked about the function of a common object, the child will be able to discriminate between an absurd and an appropriate use of the object.

The child is asked to

	First appears in
• answer questions about absurd and appropriate uses of common objects.	Lesson 125
• identify the absurd use of an object in a picture and explain why it is absurd.	Lesson 125

   For example—It would be absurd to use a pencil to brush your teeth.

Behavioral Objectives—Parts
When shown pictures of a common object, the child is able to discriminate between correct parts and absurd parts of the object.

The child is asked to

	First appears in
• name the correct parts of a pictured object and discuss the functions of these parts.	Lesson 127

- identify an inappropriate part of a pictured object and explain why its presence is absurd.   Lesson 127

  For example—It would be absurd to have legs on a wagon. It can't move without wheels.

Behavioral Objectives—Location

When asked about a location, the child is able to discriminate between things that would be appropriate and things that would be absurd in the location.

The child is asked to   *First appears in*
- answer questions about things that would be appropriate or absurd in a location.   Lesson 139
- identify appropriate or absurd things in a pictured location.   Lesson 139

  For example—It would be absurd to find an elephant in a grocery store.

VII. Workbook

A. Workbook Skills   Range of lessons 1–60

Purpose of the track

To teach the skills necessary to complete some workbook exercises

Behavioral Objectives—Cross-Out Marks and Circles

When given directions to cross out or circle particular pictures, the child is able to make a cross-out mark and a circle.

The child is asked to   *First appears in*
- make a cross-out mark by following dotted lines.   Lesson 1
- make a circle by following a dotted line.   Lesson 23
- make a cross-out mark or a circle.   Lesson 24

Behavioral Objectives—Matching

When shown pictures of objects in two columns, the child is able to match the same objects by drawing a line.

The child is asked to   *First appears in*
- draw a line connecting two objects that are the same.   Lesson 6

Behavioral Objectives—Picture Completion

When shown an unfinished picture, the child is able to trace the dotted line to complete the picture.

The child is asked to   *First appears in*
- follow a dotted line to complete a picture.   Lesson 42

B. Colors   Range of lessons 1–120

Purpose of the track

To teach the child the concept of color and to recognize colors

Behavioral Objectives

When the teacher names a color, the child is able to select the appropriate crayon, color specified objects, and name the color.

The child is asked to recognize and name the following colors:

	First appears in			*First appears in*
yellow	Lesson 14		green	Lesson 51
red	Lesson 17		brown	Lesson 62
blue	Lesson 23		pink	Lesson 113
black	Lesson 39		purple	Lesson 117
orange	Lesson 47			

C. Shapes/Draw Figures

Range of lessons 62–137

Purpose of the track
To teach the child the concept of shape and to recognize and draw shapes

Behavioral Objectives—Recognition of Shapes
When the teacher names a shape, the child is able to recognize a picture of the shape and discriminate between shapes by coloring each a different color.

The child is asked to recognize and color the following shapes:

	First appears in			*First appears in*
triangle	Lesson 62		rectangle	Lesson 83
circle	Lesson 65		square	Lesson 90

Behavioral Objectives—Draw Figures
When pictures of a shape are presented, the child is able to recognize the shape and complete the unfinished shapes by following the dots.

The child is asked to

First appears in
• follow a dotted line to complete a shape.   Lesson 83

VIII. Storybook

Range of lessons 21–150

Purpose of the track
To give the child an opportunity to comprehend stories and poems

Behavioral Objectives
1. **When presented with a story read aloud, the child is able to follow the sequence of events that occurs in the story and respond to questions and instructions about the story.**

The child is asked to

First appears in

• follow the story and the sequence of events that occur in a story that is read aloud.   Lesson 21

• respond to questions and instructions about the story.   Lesson 21

2. **When presented with a poem or nursery rhyme, the child is able to respond to questions about the reading and recite the poem or nursery rhyme.**

The child is asked to

First appears in

• respond to questions about a poem or nursery rhyme.   Lesson 24

• recite a poem or nursery rhyme.   Lesson 24